My Name is James

A Collection of Stories about People who Share my Name

By Allison Dearstyne

"I was never content unless I was trying my skill… or testing my endurance."
— Jim Thorpe

Dedicated to every boy named James. May you be content, build skills and endurance all your life.

The name James comes from the Hebrew name Jacob. Like the name Jacob, the name James means "supplanter" or "he grabs the heel." The meaning comes from the story in the Torah and the Bible of baby Jacob grabbing his older twin brother Esau's heel as they were born. Later Jacob tricked Esau into trading his future inheritance for a dinner. A supplanter is someone who takes the place of someone who was there first, just like Jacob in the Torah and the Bible.

The name Jacob, when translated into Latin, is Iacobus or Iacomus, which became James. There are several men named James in the Bible, including two disciples and a brother of Jesus who wrote a letter to the early church. Historically, James has been a common name for kings and the most popular name for American Presidents. Who knows, maybe you will be next!

There are many wonderful people in history who have shared your name. We will look at these seven outstanding men named James who changed their world, just like you will:

James "Jim" Thorpe
James Madison
James Wong Howe
James Earl Jones
James Naismith
James McCune Smith
James Stewart

James "Jim" Thorpe was an American Indian star athlete and Olympic Gold Medalist. Born in 1887 in present-day Oklahoma, Jim Thorpe grew up on an Indian reservation with his family. He was part Fox and part Sauk Indian. His American Indian name was Wa-Tho-Huk, which means "Bright Path." His childhood was marked by several tragedies. His twin brother Charlie died when they were nine years old, his mother died two years after that, and his father died when he was a teenager.

He moved to Pennsylvania, where he attended Carlisle Indian Industrial School. One day while walking by the track, Jim Thorpe did an impromptu jump over a five-foot-nine pole in street clothes! That was the beginning of his athletic career. A coach at his school recognized his talent and became a mentor to him. He won competitions in track, high jumping, football, lacrosse, baseball, and even ballroom dancing!

Jim Thorpe was most famous for his athleticism in track and field, but his favorite sport was football. He began training for the 1912 Summer Olympics in Sweden just a few months before it took place. During his training, he added some new skills: pole-vaulting, discus, javelin, and hammer. He used these skills to compete in the decathlon and the pentathlon, which are two multi-event competitions.

Just before the decathlon, someone stole his shoes! Resourceful Jim Thorpe rummaged around in a few trash cans to find shoes so he could compete. After finding two mismatched shoes in the garbage, he went on to win the gold in both events! Jim Thorpe won eight of the 15 individual events that made up the pentathlon and the decathlon.

When awarding Jim Thorpe his medal, King Gustav of Sweden said, "You, sir, are the greatest athlete in the world."

Jim Thorpe humbly replied, "Thanks, King."

After winning the gold in both events, Jim Thorpe and some other American athletes played in an exhibition game of baseball against Sweden. The purpose of the game was to introduce the world to the American sport by demonstrating how it was played. The public would soon learn that Jim Thorpe had played baseball before as a paid gig, which would lead him to be stripped of all his Olympic Medals. It wasn't fair! This is how all his medals were taken from him:

In 1912, there were strict rules in place about being an amateur in sports. That means athletes were not allowed to compete in the Olympics if they had previously played for money. Jim Thorpe had previously played baseball for a small amount of money and at the time of the Olympics, he did not know about this rule. College athletes often used fake names when they played for money so that they could compete in the Olympics, and Jim Thorpe always used his real name. He was stripped of all his medals and awards by committee members who broke a rule themselves by taking these honors away from him. For years, Jim Thorpe's fans tried to have the decision reversed and finally they succeeded - in 1983, 30 years after his death.

One positive thing from the incident was that professional baseball teams all wanted Jim Thorpe as a player. Throughout his baseball career, he played for the New York Giants, the Milwaukee Brewers, and the Cincinnati Reds. But while he played for those teams, Jim Thorpe was paraded and made to dress up in traditional American Indian clothes to be a sideshow for spectators. It was insulting. He faced racism by reporters and sportswriters throughout his baseball career.

During the years he played professional baseball, he also played professional football for the Bulldogs, one of 14 teams that formed the American Professional Football Association. Later this organization was called the National Football League, or the NFL, and Jim Thorpe was its first president. During his years of playing professional baseball and football, Jim Thorpe also played professional basketball, but many of his records were not well-documented.

Jim Thorpe was one of the greatest athletes ever! ABC sports has named him the number one athlete of the 20th century because he was so good at so many sports. If you play any American sport, there is a good chance that Jim Thorpe not only played it but dominated in it!

He said, "I have always liked sport and only played or run races for the fun of the thing." Whether or not you are an athlete, decide to enjoy yourself while you play sports with your friends and you can be like Jim Thorpe!

James Madison was a little man who made a big difference in United States history! He was born in Virginia in 1751, the oldest of 12 children. Growing up, James Madison was wealthy and well-educated, but frail. As an adult, he stood five feet tall and never weighed more than 100 pounds. When he attended present-day Princeton University, he became a talented writer, speaker and debater. Those skills would later help form a new nation.

The American Revolution against Britain began when James Madison was a young man. He served as a political leader in Virginia, but he was too sickly to be a soldier. He played an important role in protecting religious freedom in his state and later in his country. When the American Revolution was won, the new nation struggled under a weak system of government called the Articles of Confederation. It was clear to James Madison that some huge improvements needed to be made.

He wrote, "a crisis had arrived which was to decide whether the American experiment was to be a blessing to the world, or to blast forever the hopes which the republican cause had inspired."

It was James Madison's idea to scrap the Articles of Confederation altogether and create a whole new Constitution at the Philadelphia Convention in 1787. His friends George Washington, Thomas Jefferson, Alexander Hamilton and many others attended the Convention and gave their input. Writing the new successful Constitution of the United States was a team effort but it was James Madison who took the lead in debates, recorded the unofficial minutes of the meetings, and later fought hard for the Bill of Rights to be added to it. For these reasons, James Madison earned the title "Father of the Constitution."

Later he married Dolley Payne Todd, served as Secretary of State, and was elected President. During his Presidency, more trouble arose between Britain and the United States. The War of 1812 began between them. The United States lacked money and had some weak generals leading the Army. During the war, the British burned the White House to the ground, but not before Dolley rescued the prized portrait of George Washington. Despite many setbacks, the United States once again defeated Britain, boosting morale nationwide. Francis Scott Key wrote the United States' national anthem, "The Star-Spangled Banner," in a moment of great pride at the war's end!

James Madison's greatest claim to fame was his matchless role as a champion for the United States Constitution. Without it, the United States may have been doomed. The next time you see an American flag, give it a salute and think about Founding Father James Madison!

James Wong Howe was a Chinese American cinematographer who worked on over 130 films throughout his long career. In 1899 he was born Wong Tung Jim in Guangzhou, China. When he was five, he emigrated with his family to the United States and grew up in Washington. As a boy, James was given a Brownie camera, which was a cheap cardboard box camera. It sparked an early interest in photography for James Wong Howe.

When he grew up, he got a low-paying job in a film lab. To earn extra money, he snapped portraits of Hollywood stars. During one of these sessions, he took a still shot of a silent film star, Mary Miles Minters, who had very pale eyes. James Wong Howe found that he could make her eyes look darker in photographs if she looked at a darker surface. She loved the effect and requested that he direct photography as first cameraman on her next feature! He placed a large black velvet frame around the camera to produce the same effect in film.

James Wong Howe kept improving cinematography! He was the first person to film with a camera on a wheeled cart, or dolly. He even wore roller skates to capture scenes in clever ways! In the early days of his career, films were silent. In 1927, the first "talkie," or film with sound, was introduced. This new technology in film pushed James Wong Howe to change his techniques too, and in the 1930s he reestablished himself as one of the leading cinematographers in Hollywood. He won several Academy Awards.

Throughout his life, James Wong Howe experienced racial discrimination. He was not allowed to become an American citizen until 1943, when a racist law against Chinese Americans was overturned. Overseas he married a White woman named Sanora Babb, but their marriage was not legally recognized by the United States for 11 years because they were an interracial couple. Despite these hardships, they remained happily married.

James Wong Howe wasn't afraid to try new things in filmmaking. The next time you film something, think outside the box about your technique and you can be like creative James Wong Howe!

James Earl Jones was a Black American actor best known for his deep, thunderous voice. He was born in 1931 in Mississippi to parents with Black, Irish, Choctaw and Cherokee ancestry. He faced several hardships during his childhood. His father left his family when he was a baby, and he moved to Michigan a few years later to be raised by his grandparents.

James Earl Jones described his grandmother as "the most racist person I have ever known," having a "double-edged contempt for White folk." As he grew up, he knew he had to break free of that way of thinking. His move to Michigan was so traumatic for him that he began stuttering. The problem became so severe that he refused to speak at all for eight years. As an adult, James Earl Jones spoke about his struggle with stuttering.

He said, "One of the hardest things in life is having words in your heart that you can't utter." Thankfully, a kind schoolteacher helped him overcome his stuttering when he discovered that James Earl Jones had a gift for writing poetry. His teacher encouraged him to write poems and recite them for his classmates. James Earl Jones finally began speaking again when he was in high school, and later he majored in drama at the University of Michigan. After he graduated, he moved to New York, where he acted on Broadway. He became a great success and then began acting in movies.

His most famous role has been his voice-over for the villain, Darth Vader, in the *Star Wars* series. He is also the voice of wise Mufasa in Disney's *The Lion King*, and he plays Mr. Mertle in *The Sandlot*. His laughter is contagious, and his booming voice is recognizable to almost everyone. That is quite impressive for being a boy who stuttered!

James Earl Jones had the distinction of being an "EGOT," which means he has received at least one of all the four major entertainment awards; an Emmy, a Grammy, an Oscar, and a Tony. Only 27 people in the world are "EGOTs."

Whenever you hear James Earl Jones' booming voice, be inspired by his wonderful story of how much he overcame!

James Naismith was the Canadian American who invented basketball. He was born in 1861 in Ontario to Scottish immigrants. As a little boy, James struggled in school but loved to play outside. His favorite game was called "duck on a rock," which is a game where one person guards a large stone from people who try to knock it down by throwing stones at it. While he played, he came up with a new method of taking a soft lobbing shot at the large stone. It was much more effective than the straight hard throws that the other children tried. It turns out that this insight later proved important in his invention of basketball!

James Naismith was orphaned as a boy and was raised by his aunt and uncle. He graduated from McGill University and became a physical education teacher at a YMCA, or Young Men's Christian Association, in Massachusetts. At the YMCA, James Naismith struggled with teaching a rowdy group of boys who were bored by indoor games during the long winter. His supervisor told him he had two weeks to create a fun indoor game for those rascally boys. He required that the game not take up much room, help track athletes to stay in shape, and not be too rough.

James Naismith remembered his favorite childhood game "duck on a rock" and combined it with ideas from popular sports. He used a soccer ball, tied peach baskets high onto a wall, and allowed nine players on each team. To make it safe, passing the ball was the only legal way to move it around the court. He explained the rules to the boys and blew the whistle to begin. The first basketball game was a total disaster! The boys began tackling, kicking, and punching each other in the middle of the gym floor. After just a few minutes of playing, there were several black eyes, one separated shoulder, and one player knocked unconscious.

James Naismith knew he had some more work to do! He came up with ways to improve his game and within a year, basketball became wildly popular. When James Naismith saw basketball demonstrated in the 1904 Summer Olympics, he said that seeing his game played by many nations was the greatest reward he could have for his invention.

Those who knew James Naismith said he was a great listener and a wonderful man. The next time your friends or family are playing basketball, join in and think about James Naismith!

James McCune Smith was a Black American physician, pharmacist, abolitionist and author. He had mixed ancestry and was born a slave in 1813 in New York City. He was raised by his mother and freed in 1827, when slavery became illegal in New York. As a boy, James McCune Smith was exceptionally smart. After graduating from high school, he found that he would not be accepted at his local schools of choice because of his race. But that didn't stop him! He was accepted at the University of Glasgow in Scotland, and several of his high school teachers paid for his education overseas. He graduated at the top of his class with a medical degree.

When he returned to the United States, he married Malvina Barnet and together they had 11 children. He became a great success in his career as the first university-trained Black American physician in the United States. During his 25 years working as a doctor, he treated both Black and White patients. He opened the first Black-owned pharmacy in the United States. The back room of the pharmacy became a meeting place for his Black and White friends to work together in abolitionism, which is ending slavery altogether.

His good friend Frederick Douglass said that James McCune Smith was the single most influential person in his life! Abolitionist meetings would sometimes get heated, and arguments broke out. But James McCune Smith was a peacemaker, calmly insisting on debating from facts, not emotion. Following this belief, James McCune Smith wrote a lot of articles on abolishing slavery and on medical topics too. He was considered one of the great intellectuals of his time.

In history, James McCune Smith has been an unsung hero, and that is largely because of poor record-keeping in his day. Historic documents often wrongly identified James McCune Smith as being White. For over a century, this wrong record remained uncorrected. But in recent years, his great-great-great granddaughter found his name in a family Bible, which led historians to properly identify James McCune Smith as being mixed race. His descendants gave him a new tombstone in 2010 which honored and correctly identified him.

We learn from James McCune Smith to accomplish things through a calm, level-headed approach. When you face a conflict with others, choose to be a peacemaker like James McCune Smith!

James Stewart was an American actor and military officer with a slow drawl and a big heart. He was born in Pennsylvania in 1908 and called Jimmy, a nickname that stuck with him for life. His father ran a store, and it was expected that young James would continue the family business when he grew up.

After graduating from high school, he majored in architecture at Princeton University. He did so well that he was awarded a scholarship for graduate school, but he began to love acting and turned down the scholarship to try a different career. While James Stewart was in college, the stock market crashed, and Americans everywhere lost a lot of money. Jobs were scarce, especially for a rising actor like James Stewart. Nevertheless, after he graduated, he began his acting career in Broadway productions.

Most plays he acted in closed or got bad reviews, but he alone was praised by critics for his acting ability. Gangly and humble, James Stewart started with small roles in plays, but the audience loved him. His friend Henry Fonda helped him make connections in Hollywood to act in movies. As his career in movies began, so did World War II. James Stewart became a star, won his first Academy Award, and then life changed again for Americans when the United States was attacked by Japan at Pearl Harbor. James Stewart bravely enlisted in the Army and was rejected because he was too skinny. So, he exercised to build his muscles and joined as a pilot, becoming the first major American movie star to be a soldier in World War II.

His skill and bravery during the war got him promoted from private to colonel in only four years! Decades later, President Ronald Reagan awarded James Stewart the Presidential Medal of Freedom for his service. After the war, he starred in a movie you often see on TV around Christmastime, *It's a Wonderful Life*. Playing the part of George Bailey defined James Stewart as an actor. The movie was at first a flop but was later ranked in the 100 best American movies ever made.

A few years later, he married Gloria McLean, adopted her two sons and then had twin daughters. He adored his family and was described by everyone who knew him as kind and soft-spoken. James Stewart said that he wanted to be remembered as someone who believed in hard work, love of country, love of family, and love of community. He certainly is remembered for all those things!

Quiet, heroic James Stewart succeeded as an actor for 60 years! This Christmas, watch *It's a Wonderful Life* and think about talented James Stewart!

This page is all about you!

_____ was born on

_____

As a baby, James _____

_____

As a little boy, James _____

_____

James is especially good at _____

_____

James is often described as _____

_____

James makes people laugh when he _____

_____

One day James would like to _____

_____

This page is for making a self-portrait. A self-portrait is a picture of you, drawn by you!

Bibliography

Biography.com editors. "James Naismith Biography." The Biography.com website. A&E Television Networks. 4 Nov. 2017. Web. 30 Nov. 2018.

Encyclopaedia Britannica Editors. "James Wong Howe." *Encyclopaedia Britannica.* Encyclopaedia Britannica, inc. 24 Aug. 2018. Web. 14 Dec. 2018.

Encyclopaedia Britannica Editors. "James Earl Jones." *Encyclopaedia Britannica.* Encyclopaedia Britannica, inc. 15 Nov 2018. Web. 26 Nov. 2018.

Encyclopaedia Britannica Editors. "James Naismith." *Encyclopaedia Britannica.* Encyclopaedia Britannica, inc. 24 Nov 2018. Web. 30 Nov. 2018.

Encyclopaedia Britannica Editors. "James Stewart." *Encyclopaedia Britannica.* Encyclopaedia Britannica, inc. 28 Jun. 2018. Web. 03 Dec. 2018.

Encyclopaedia Britannica Editors. "Jim Thorpe." *Encyclopaedia Britannica.* Encyclopaedia Britannica, inc. 28 May 2018. Web. 2 Nov. 2018.

Brant, Irving. "James Madison." *Encyclopaedia Britannica.* Encyclopaedia Britannica, inc. 26 Oct. 2018. Web. 06 Dec. 2018.

Wikipedia contributors. "James Wong Howe." *Wikipedia, The Free Encyclopedia.* Wikipedia, The Free Encyclopedia, 16 Nov. 2018. Web. 14 Dec. 2018.

Wikipedia contributors. "James Earl Jones." *Wikipedia, The Free Encyclopedia*. Wikipedia, The Free Encyclopedia, 24 Nov. 2018. Web. 26 Nov. 2018.

Wikipedia contributors. "James Naismith." *Wikipedia, The Free Encyclopedia*. Wikipedia, The Free Encyclopedia, 30 Nov. 2018. Web. 30 Nov. 2018.

Wikipedia contributors. "James Madison." *Wikipedia, The Free Encyclopedia*. Wikipedia, The Free Encyclopedia, 2 Dec. 2018. Web. 6 Dec. 2018.

Wikipedia contributors. "James McCune Smith." *Wikipedia, The Free Encyclopedia*. Wikipedia, The Free Encyclopedia, 1 Dec. 2018. Web. 6 Dec. 2018.

Wikipedia contributors. "James Stewart." *Wikipedia, The Free Encyclopedia*. Wikipedia, The Free Encyclopedia, 2 Dec. 2018. Web. 3 Dec. 2018.

Wikipedia contributors. "Jim Thorpe." *Wikipedia, The Free Encyclopedia*. Wikipedia, The Free Encyclopedia, 2 Nov. 2018. Web. 2 Nov. 2018.

Winter, Kari J. "Smith, James McCune (1813-1865)." BlackPast.org Remembered & Reclaimed. 2017. Web. 5 Dec. 2018.

www.ingramcontent.com/pod-product-compliance
Lightning Source LLC
Chambersburg PA
CBHW042111040426
42448CB00002B/224